WHERE'S WALLY?
THE SEARCH FOR THE LOST THINGS
WIZARD WHITEBEARD'S SCROLL

MARTIN HANDFORD

Walker Books
AND SUBSIDIARIES
LONDON · BOSTON · SYDNEY · AUCKLAND

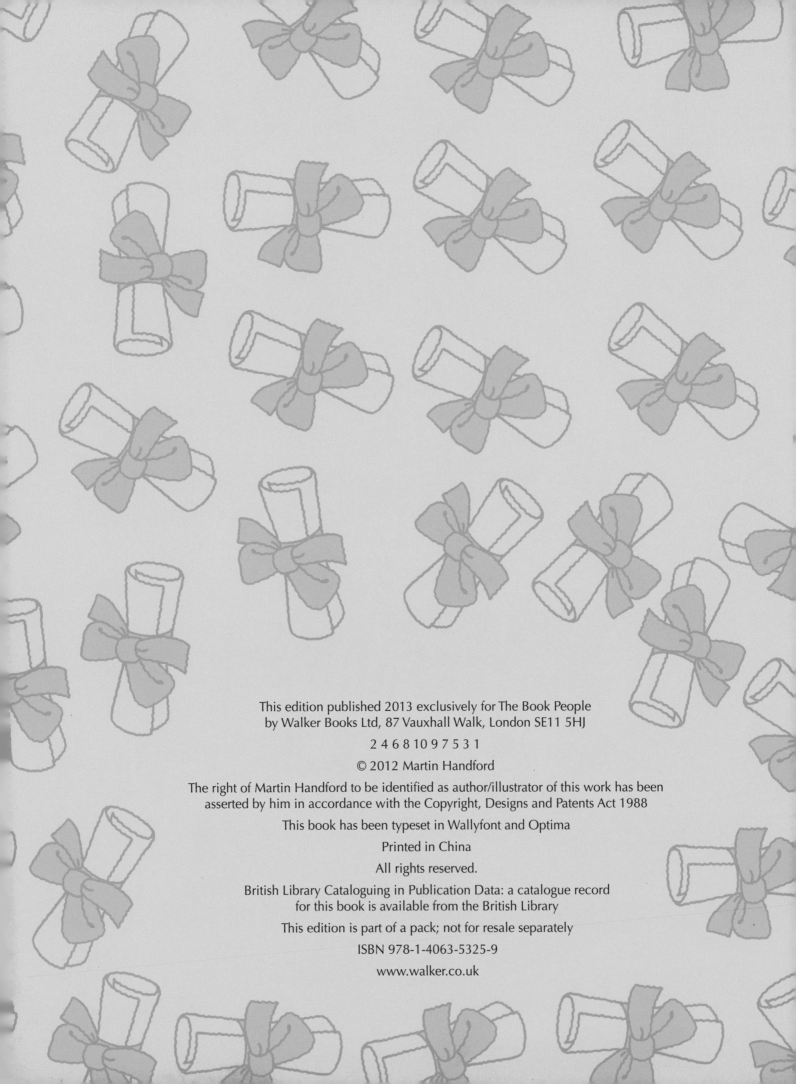

This edition published 2013 exclusively for The Book People
by Walker Books Ltd, 87 Vauxhall Walk, London SE11 5HJ

2 4 6 8 10 9 7 5 3 1

© 2012 Martin Handford

The right of Martin Handford to be identified as author/illustrator of this work has been
asserted by him in accordance with the Copyright, Designs and Patents Act 1988

This book has been typeset in Wallyfont and Optima

Printed in China

All rights reserved.

British Library Cataloguing in Publication Data: a catalogue record
for this book is available from the British Library

This edition is part of a pack; not for resale separately

ISBN 978-1-4063-5325-9

www.walker.co.uk

GREETINGS, WISE ONES,

SWISH! ZAP! ... POOF! CRUMBS, I'VE CAST A SPELL THAT'S MADE
MY RED-RIBBONED SCROLL DISAPPEAR. HOW ON EARTH DID
THAT MAGICAL MUDDLE HAPPEN? BOTHER! AND WHERE DID ALL
THOSE BLUE-RIBBONED SCROLLS COME FROM?

JOIN ME ON MY QUEST TO SEEK OUT MY PRECIOUS SCROLL
AND RECOVER THE 16 BLUE-RIBBONED ONES BEFORE IT TURNS
INTO CATACLYSMIC CHAOS!

AND THERE'S MORE! TWO OF THESE WALLY WATCHERS ARE
WANDERING THROUGH THIS BOOK. CAN YOU FIND THEM?

I'D LOSE MY HEAD IF IT WASN'T
ATTACHED TO MY BEARD!

Whitebeard

WIZARD
WHITEBEARD'S
SCROLL

BLUE-RIBBONED
SCROLL

STARS AND STRIPES

Which stripy path leads from Wizard Whitebeard's seal to his star? You better get there quickly as his spell is making multiple Wallies!

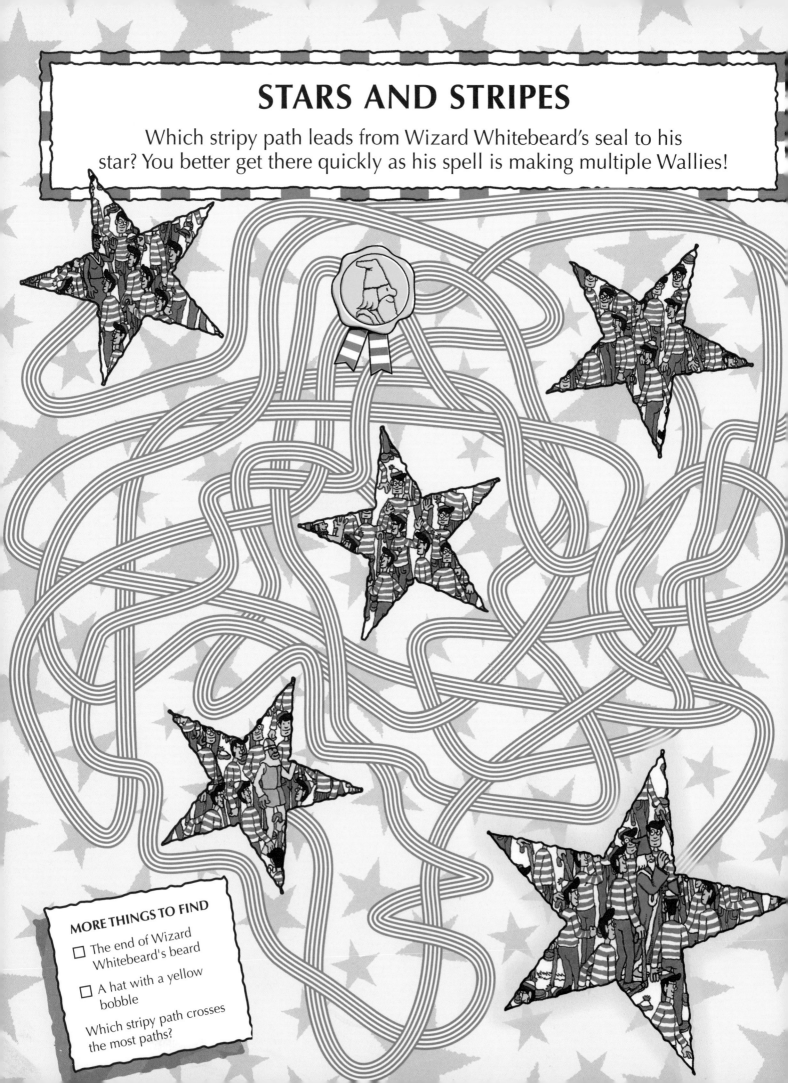

SOMETHING FISHY

Match up the sets of three identically coloured fish. One fish is not part of a set, so have a splish-splashing time finding out which one!

MORE THINGS TO FIND

☐ A smiling fish

☐ An angry fish

☐ A fish with closed eyes

SPELL-TACULAR!

These four words have stretched out in a spectacular star shape.
Can you train your eyes to read them?

START HERE!

MORE THINGS TO FIND

☐ A white suitcase

☐ A stripy rocket

☐ A green wellington boot

☐ A frog

Clue: hold the book in front of your nose and tilt it backwards. Read the word in front of you, then turn the book to the right and read the next word and so on.

GIANT GAME

Start on the board game square next to each player's picture.
Then follow their footstep guide to work out who picks up the scroll.

MORE THINGS TO FIND
- ☐ Nine men wearing helmets
- ☐ Someone wearing blue and yellow tights
- ☐ Four pitch forks

MIX-UP MADNESS

What a muddle! Match the top halves of these characters to the correct bottom halves.

MORE THINGS TO DO

* Draw your own fantasy characters in the two blank boxes! Flick through the book for inspiration for a top half and a bottom half.

* Give some of the mixed-up characters combination names e.g. Vikingator (viking + gladiator).

TWO BY TWO

Wizard Whitebeard is helping Noah get pairs of animals on to his ark. Join up the numbered red dots to reveal a creature that wants to travel alone.

MORE THINGS TO FIND
- [ ] An elephant shaped tree
- [ ] Another Noah's ark in this chapter
- [ ] A bird's nest

WORD CASTLE

Find the words at the bottom of this page in the three-letter bricks of this castle. A word can read across more than one brick.

R	O	F		A	R	A	M	I	D	A	X	E
M	X	A		J	O	P	W	W	O		W	G	R
L	W	A	D	R	A	W	B	R	I	D	G	E	H	L	D	R	A
F	L	A	G	L	V	N	E	K	R	C	A	T	A	P	U	L	T
N	T	P	C	A	S	T	L	E	L	Q	P	U	F	M	P	X	E
W	Q	T	E	U	F	Y	U	X	H	D	A	B	A	T	T	L	E
M	O	A	T	H	Y	K	W	S	E	J	I	U	L	E	I	A	F
D	G	E	M	I	L	A	I	N	S	I	F	O	R	T	A	F	R
A	R	R	O	W	H	R	E	E	A	K	L	K	C	E	T	L	H
H	F	M	A	R	A	W	N	P	M	T	L	H	F	L	A	G	T
W	A	L	L	T	O	H	Y	O	E	A	B	O	W	P	P	C	G

MORE THINGS TO FIND

☐ A word that features twice in the puzzle

☐ Two magic words that can open the castle drawbridge.

Clue: ten letters that go up, across and down.

O _ _ _ _ / _ _ S _ _ E

BOW
WALL
MOAT
ARROW
CASTLE
DRAWBRIDGE

CATAPULT
RAM
FORT
AXE
BATTLE
FLAG

SHIELDS AND STAVES

On guard, eyes at the ready! Find two pictures that are the same.

MORE THINGS TO FIND

Which colour frames are there most of?

☐ Four blue shields

☐ Eight green hats

☐ A carved red staff

☐ A man with stars above his head

GENIE-OUS!

Draw in the missing symbols to release the genie from its lamp!
All nine symbols must appear once in each box,
but never in the same row.

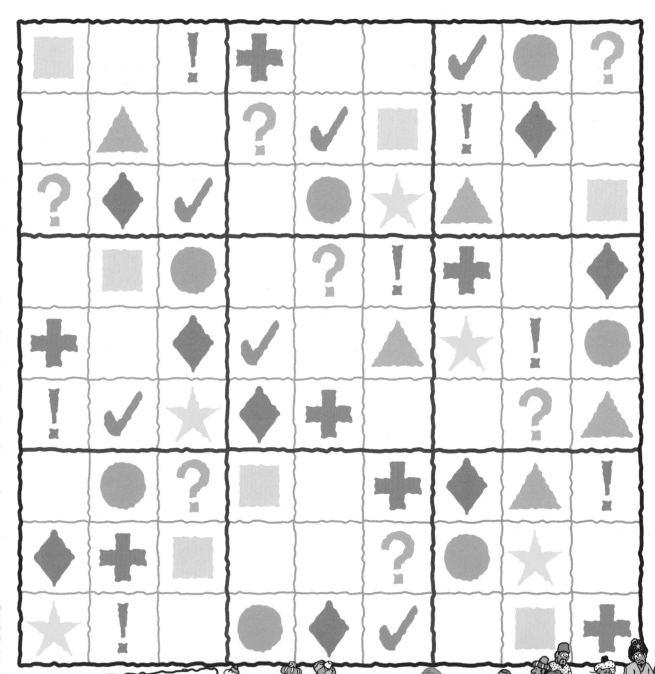

DOUBLE VISION

All is not what it seems with these magic monks and red-cloaked ghouls.
Spot six differences in one of the scenes.

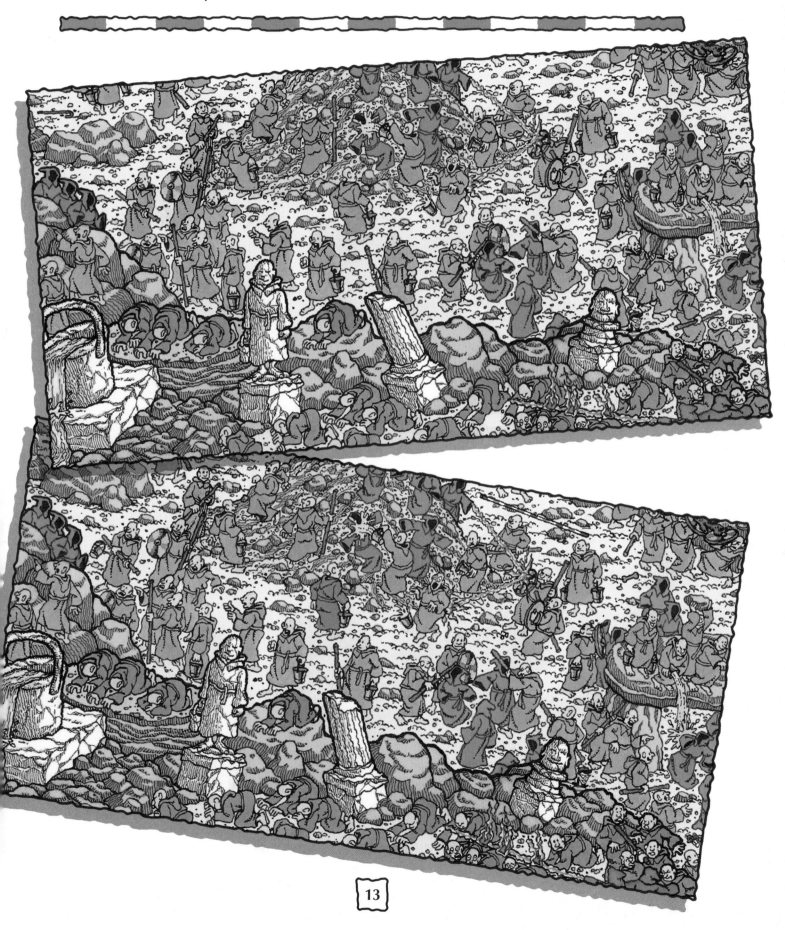

FRUIT SQUASH

Study the fruit in the puzzle closely – to the left and right, above and below. There are two *zesty* fruit which are always next to each other. Can you draw them in the empty squares?

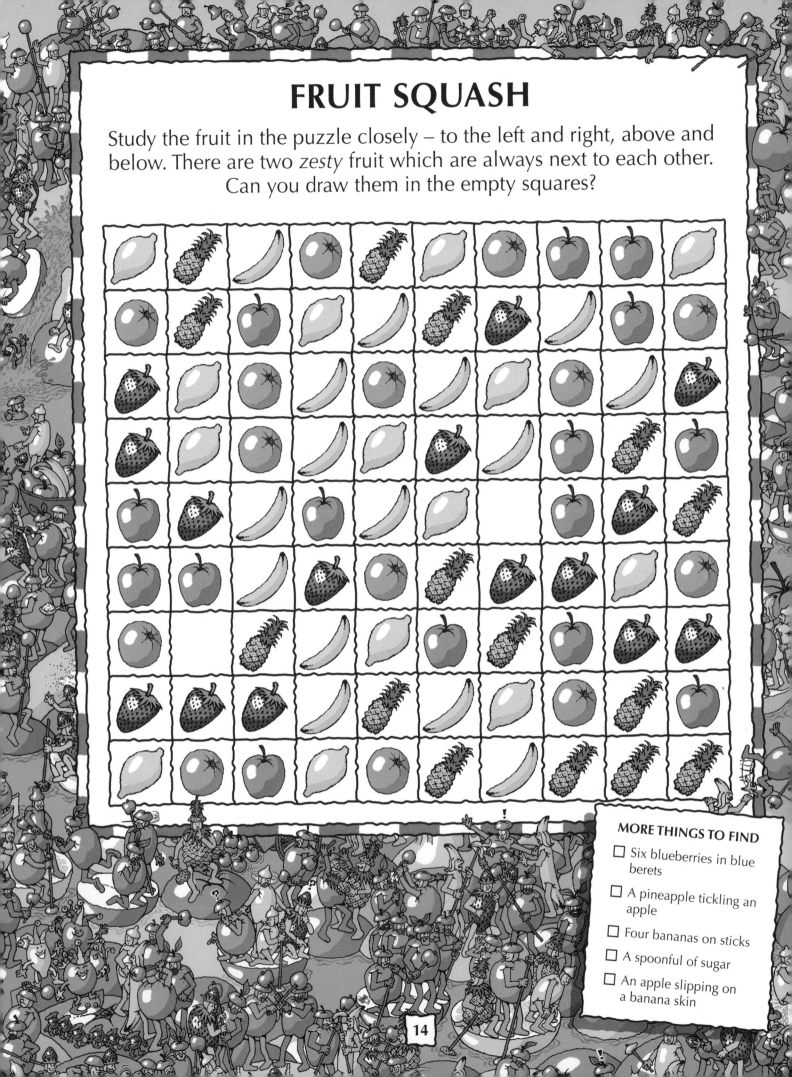

DRAGON DELIGHT

A magical dragon flying competition is about to begin. Draw lots of other dragon contestants to take part in it!

MORE THINGS TO DO

Choose your favourite dragon (it might be one that you have drawn) and give it a name. What do you think its eggs look like and what is its favourite food?

Look at the picture and find:

☐ A dragon with a very long tail

☐ A dragon egg

☐ A red spotty bag on a stick

HAT TRICK

Wow! Pow! Kazam! Draw tiny people underneath
the hats to create your own scene.

MORE THINGS TO DO

★ Draw in Wally, Wizard
Whitebeard and Odlaw
underneath their hats.

★ Make your own wizard hat!

WHICH WITCH IS WHICH?

Read the witchy riddles and match them to the pictures.

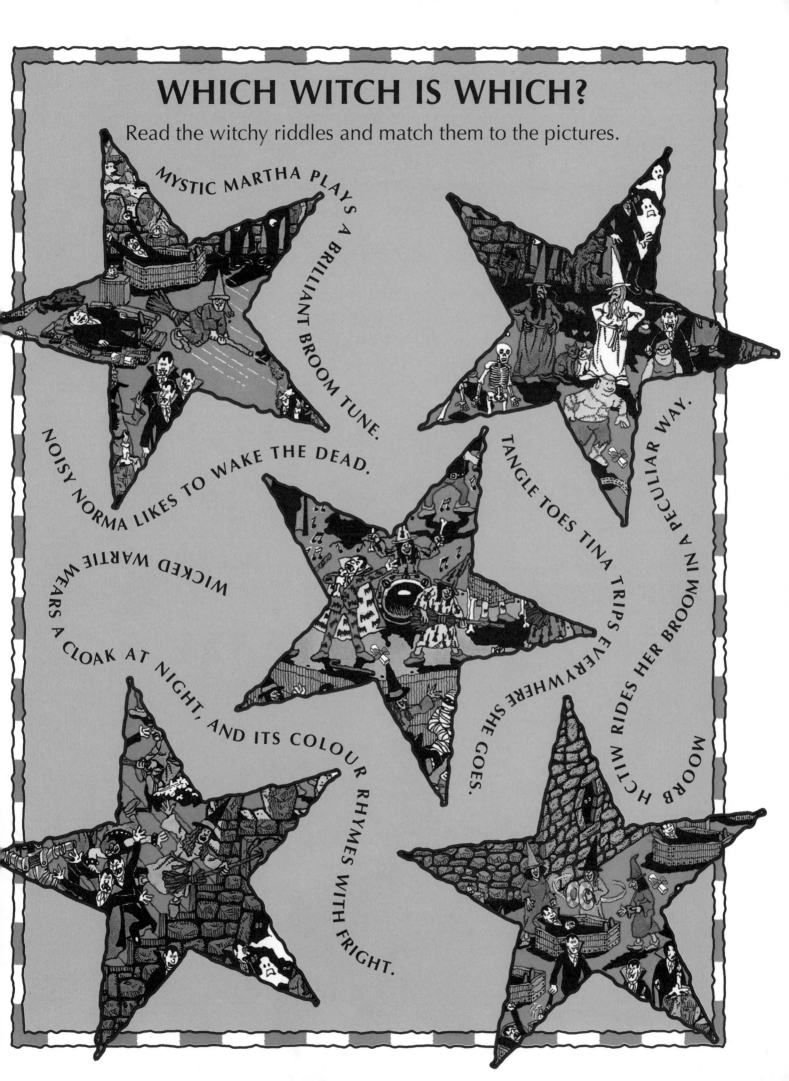

MYSTIC MARTHA PLAYS A BRILLIANT BROOM TUNE.

NOISY NORMA LIKES TO WAKE THE DEAD.

WICKED WARTIE WEARS A CLOAK AT NIGHT, AND ITS COLOUR RHYMES WITH FRIGHT.

TANGLE TOES TINA TRIPS EVERYWHERE SHE GOES.

WITCH ROBBY RIDES HER BROOM IN A PECULIAR WAY.

MAGIC NUMBER

Cross out the numbers in the border
matching these descriptions and reveal
a magic number to be used later...

☆ Number sevens

☆ Two numbers next
to each other that
are the same

☆ Two numbers next
to each other that
add up to ten

☆ Even numbers

MORE THINGS TO FIND

☐ 11 bears

☐ A kangaroo

☐ Two astronauts

☐ A magic star wand

WISE CRACKS

Wizard Whitebeard has cast a happy spell! This scroll is inscribed with lots of jokes. Which one makes you laugh the most?

WHAT'S SO SPECIAL ABOUT THE WAY WIZARDS SERVE THEIR TEA?

THEY GIVE YOU BISCUITS ON A FLYING SORCERER!

HOW MANY WIZARDS DOES IT TAKE TO CAST A SPELL OF INVISIBILITY?

I DON'T KNOW, I CAN'T SEE THEM!

HOW BEST TO DESCRIBE A WIZARD'S BOOK?

SPELL-BINDING!

WHY CAN'T WIZARDS CLEAN FLOORS?

BECAUSE THE WITCHES STOLE THEIR BROOMS!

WHAT DO YOU CALL A LAUGHING POTION?

MAKES-YOU-GIGGLE-A-LOT-IOUS!

MORE THINGS TO DO
* Make up your own joke in the space on the scroll and test it on your friends.
* Try out five different laughs!

....

....

....

STUPENDOUS SORCERERS! I'M STILL DISCOMBOBULATED ABOUT WHERE MY MAGIC SCROLL IS HIDING. I HOPE I DIDN'T TURN IT INVISIBLE! DID YOU SPOT IT AND THE IMPRESSIVE NUMBER OF BLUE-RIBBONED SCROLLS I CREATED?

I'VE CONJURED UP A RIDDLE CLUE TO FOCUS OUR MINDS: SEEK OUT A MAN WITH A LONG WHITE BEARD AND ABOVE HIM A HANGING SIGN. THE SCROLL IS BUT A WHISKER AWAY!

Whitebeard

A mermaid's tail

Candle wax

A bird's nest

Wizard Whitebeard needs an able apprentice to find these special spell ingredients. Look through this book and gather them as fast as you can!

A genie's earring

A jest of lemon

A dragon egg

WIZARD WHITEBEARD'S SCROLL CHECKLIST

Cast your eyes over Wizard Whitebeard's quest and find…

- ☐ Wizard Whitebeard in a boat
- ☐ Someone blowing a whistle
- ☐ A man wearing a bow tie
- ☐ A snake shaking maracas
- ☐ A flag with five faces
- ☐ A sea lion
- ☐ Nine gold crowns
- ☐ A windmill
- ☐ Someone rolling a die
- ☐ Three wicker baskets
- ☐ Four jumping fish
- ☐ A gargoyle breathing fire
- ☐ A toy in a teacup
- ☐ Three genies
- ☐ A zebra crossing
- ☐ A red man that has jumped through a shield
- ☐ A wishing well
- ☐ A skeleton

ONE LAST THING…

How many stars can you find in this book (the star bullet points in the *More Things To Do* boxes don't count)?

That was sheer wizardry, well done!

Thanks for tracking down my magic scroll – I'd be in a spell-fuddled muddle without it!

There are answers to some of the trickiest puzzles over the page. Don't give up on the others – ask your friends to help if you are stuck.

ANSWERS

Pg 4 STARS AND STRIPES

The path marked in yellow leads to Wizard Whitebeard's star.

MORE THINGS TO FIND
The path in blue crosses the most paths.

Pg 5 SOMETHING FISHY

Pg 6 SPELL-TACULAR!

Magic makes much mayhem

Pg 7 GIANT GAME

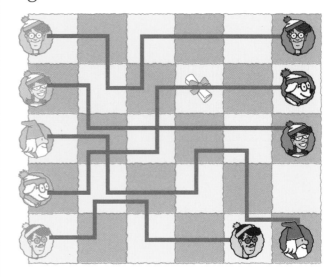

Pg 8 MIX-UP MADNESS

Pg 10 WORD CASTLE

R	O	F			A	R	A	M	I	D			A	X	E
M	X	A			J	O	P	W	W	O			W	G	R
L	W	A	D	R	A	W	B	R	I	D	G	E	D	R	A
F	L	A	G	L	V	N	E	K	R	C	A	T	A	P	U	L	T
N	T	P	C	A	S	T	L	E	L	Q	P	U	F	M	P	X	E
W	Q	T	E	U	F	Y	U	X	H	D	A	B	A	T	T	L	E
M	O	A	T	H	Y	K	W	S	E	J	I	U	L	E	I	A	F
D	G	E	M	I	L	A	I	N	S	I	F	O	R	T	A	F	R
A	R	R	O	W	H	R	E	E	A	K	L	K	C	E	T	L	H
H	F	M	A	R	A	W	N	P	M	T	L	H	F	L	A	G	T
W	A	L	L	T	O	H	Y	O	E	A	B	O	W	P	C	G

MORE THINGS TO FIND
The two magic words are 'Open Sesame'.

Pg 12 GENIE-OUS!

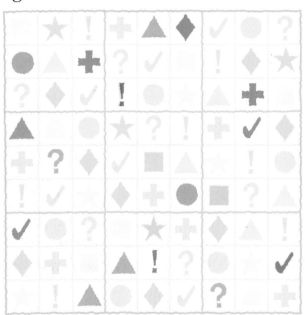

Pg 14 FRUIT SQUASH

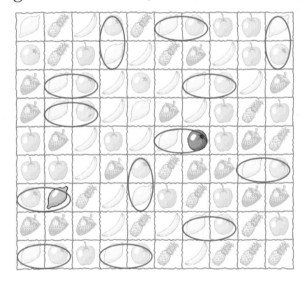

Pg 17 WHICH WITCH IS WHICH?

1. Mystic Martha plays a brilliant broom tune.
2. Noisy Norma likes to wake the dead.
3. Wicked Wartie wears a cloak at night, and its colour rhymes with fright.
4. Tangle Toes Tina trips everywhere she goes.
5. Moorb Hctiw rides her broom in a peculiar way.

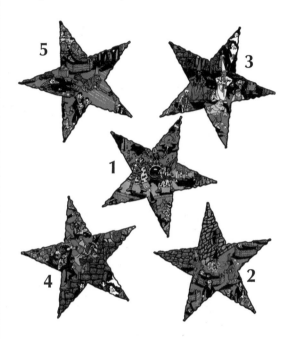

Pg 18 MAGIC NUMBER

The magic number is 5.

The adventure isn't over quite yet! After you collected the ingredients for the spell on page 20, Wizard Whitebeard magicked some gold seals which are scattered throughout the five books in this set. Can you find all the seals before Odlaw's pirate friends smuggle them away? How many are there? The answer is the magic number you found on page 18. Happy searching, Wally fans!